museum Thorvaldsens

A Guide to Thorvaldsen's Museum

museum Thorvaldsens

A Guide to Thorvaldsen's Museum

ISBN/EAN: 9783337280741

Printed in Europe, USA, Canada, Australia, Japan

Cover: Foto ©Andreas Hilbeck / pixelio.de

More available books at **www.hansebooks.com**

A GUIDE

TO

THORVALDSEN'S MUSEUM.

COPENHAGEN.

PRINTED IN THIELE'S PRESS.

1886.

Thorvaldsen's Museum was erected by the community of Copenhagen as a repository for the works of art bequeathed by Thorvaldsen to his native town, a considerable sum having been previously collected by subscription for this purpose.

Thorvaldsen's Museum is also his Mausoleum, as it contains his tomb.

The tomb is situated in the centre of the court, covered with ivy and encompassed by a granite frame on which is engraved the name BERTEL THORVALDSEN together with the dates of his birth and death: 19 November 1770, 24 March 1844. The coffin is deposited in a decorated vault built while Thorvaldsen was yet alive, and in accordance with his wishes.

The building, a work of the architect Bindesböll, was begun in 1839 and finished in 1848. In its appearance is expressed its destination as the last resting place of Thorvaldsen. The architectural style is partly borrowed from old Egyptian and Greek sepulchral buildings, and the decorations, particularly on the walls of the court, remind us of those of antique tombs. Under the windows is seen a Genius in the

Chariot-race, a symbol of the human mind tending to and reaching the goal in spite of mischance and obstacles. Intermittingly are seen vases and tripods, such as were in antiquity used as public rewards in prize contests and as offerings to the gods for victories gained; laurels, oaks, and palms, the leaves and branches of which served as emblems of honour and victory, shoot up along the walls.

The allusion to the victorious genius of Thorvaldsen is likewise observable in the decoration of the façade. Over the entrance of the museum Victory is reining up her quadriga, and in the capitals of the corner-pilasters are in front a Victory in her chariot, on the sides Sol and Luna with their swift steeds mounting to overpower darkness. The Victory in the quadriga, cast in bronze, is a present from king Christian VIII. The figure of the goddess was executed from a sketch left by Thorvaldsen, and the left of the middle horses after a model by him; the three other horses are after models by V. Bissen. The casting of the whole was executed by Dahlhoff. On the outside of the museum is represented Thorvaldsen's arrival at Copenhagen in 1838, when, after an absence of 18 years, he returned in a vessel sent out for a great part of the works destined for his museum. The arrival itself is depicted on the wall looking towards the canal, the conveyance of the works to the museum on the other side of the building. The whole of this imagery as well as that on the walls of the court has been produced by the inlaying of divers-coloured cements.

The rich decorations of the ceilings in the museum are mostly imitations from antique patterns or motives. The images forming parts of these decorations, some of them stucco-work, others paintings *al fresco*, are partly borrowed from antiques, partly copied from Thorvaldsen's works; the latter is the case in the Vestibule and in the Rooms IV, V, XV, and XVI. On the ceiling of the Room XXI are Christian representations.

The museum contains Thorvaldsen's works and collections. Besides his models and sketches in plaster and his designs, are found in the museum 109 of his works in marble, viz.: 4 groups, 20 statues, 20 busts, 65 reliefs, and 1 frieze. His works occupy the lower story and the corridors of the upper story entirely; in the latter a few of them have been placed in the rooms to the left; his sketches and designs are in the hindmost room. The models for the statues and reliefs hewn in marble are arranged in the corridor to the right in the lower story, and in the corridors at both sides in the upper story. Pictures by contemporary artists and having been possessed by Thorvaldsen are hung up in the left suit of rooms in the upper story. Antique classical art, which was of prominent interest to Thorvaldsen, is represented, in the rooms to the right, by collections of gems, coins, painted vases and various other antiquities, made during the many years of his residence at Rome, as well as by some plaster casts of antique sculptures belonging to those he had standing in his ateliers. For want of space the greater part of these casts however have been placed in the rooms of the cellar. His collections of drawings, engravings, books &c. are placed in Rooms XXXII—XLII.

In the rooms of the cellar are further to be seen: works from Thorvaldsen's youth (in XLIII), some marble statues by modern artists (in XLIV), and in the last (LIII) various things that have belonged to Thorvaldsen's effects and serve to the illustration of his person and life.

Besides this manual catalogue, to be had in the museum also in Danish, German, and French, there has been published, in Danish and in French, a complete and detailed description of the collections of the museum, consisting of 8 parts, each sold separately. 1. Thorvaldsen's works. 2. Paintings and drawings. 3. Engravings, medals, and modern sculptures. 4. Various Egyptian, Etruscan, Greek, and Roman antiquities. 5. Antique gems and pastes. 6. Antique coins. 7. Plaster casts, mostly of antiques. 8. Books and bound engravings.

The numbers of the rooms are placed under the windows.

M. is in the following catalogue added to the works of Thorvaldsen which are of marble.

L. Müller.

GROUND FLOOR.

Thorvaldsen's works.

VESTIBULE.

Colossal Statues.

113. Nicolaus Copernicus. (Model for the bronze statue at Warsaw.)

114-116. Gutenberg. On the pedestal, in relief: Invention of movable types and of the printing press. (Models for the bronze monument at Mayence.)

123. Prince Joseph Poniatowski. (Model intended for a bronze monument at Warsaw.)

128. Maximilian I, Elector of Bavaria. (Model for the bronze monument at Munich.)

135. Schiller. On the pedestal: Apotheosis of the poet; Genius of Poetry; Goddess of Victory. (Models for the bronze monument at Stuttgart.)

142-145. Pope Pius VII. To the right: Heavenly Wisdom. To the left: Divine Strength. On the pedestal: the pope's arms held by two angels. (Models for the marble monument in St. Peter's church at Rome.)

156. Eugène, duke of Leuchtenberg (In marble at. Munich on the duke's tomb.)

Colossal Busts.

209. Count A. P. Bernstorff, Danish minister.
212. Adam Moltke, count, of Nütschau.
219-220. Baron and Baroness Schubart. M.
253. Horace Vernet, the painter. M.
258. Sir Thomas Maitland, Lord Commissioner of the Ionian islands. (Modelled together with the relief No. 600 for the bronze monument in Zante.)

Reliefs.

317. Hercules receiving the drink of immortality from Hebe.
318. Hygeia feeding the serpent of Æsculapius.
319. Minerva giving a soul to the man formed by Prometheus.
320. Nemesis reading to Jupiter the deeds of men.
503. *Frieze.* Triumphal entry of Alexander the Great into Babylon. To the right: Alexander with his train. In the centre: Babylonians going in procession to meet the victor. To the left: Babylon and environs. (In the Quirinal Palace at Rome.)
530. Genius of State Government.
531. Genius of Justice.
600. Minerva protecting Virtue and unveiling Vice. (See No. 258.)

CORRIDOR.

Statues.

7. Mars and Amor. (This group together with the following statue was intended for a representation borrowed from the 45th song of Anacreon and executed in relief No. 420 opposite.)
9. Vulcanus.
52. Jason with the Golden Fleece. (First greater work by Thorvaldsen.)

55-56. Caryatides.
59-70. John the Baptist preaching. (Models for the figures placed in marble above the entrance of Our Lady's Church at Copenhagen.)
71. 72. Roman warrior, standing. Jew, sitting. (Intended for the preceding group.)
105. 108. Jude Thaddeus and Andrew, the apostles. (Modelled about 20 years after the corresponding statues in the Christus-Hall, Nos. 94 and 95, and placed, in marble, in Our Lady's Church.)
110. Angel of Baptism.
119. Lion dying over the royal shield of France. (Model for the colossal relief hewn in the side of a rock near Lucerne, in memory of the Swiss fallen in the revolt in Paris, August 10th, 1792.)
122. Couching lion.
125. Horse. (Modelled for the Poniatowski-monument.)
129. Horse. (Modelled for the monument of Maximilian I of Bavaria.)
146-147. Two angels. (For the monument of Pius VII.)
162. Thorvaldsen (in his 70eth year) leaning on the statue of Hope (see No. 46 in room VIII).

Busts.

186. St. Apollinaris, bishop of Ravenna.
187. Leonardus Pisanus, the mathematician. M.
189. Maximilian I, Elector of Bavaria.
195. Vilhelmine, Danish princess. M.
211. Count Rantzau of Breitenburg.
223. Thorvaldsen (in his 40eth year).
233. Louis I, king of Bavaria.
240. Chr. Aug. Tiedge, the poet.
247. Helena, Grand-Duchess.
252. Napoleon I, as apotheosized emperor. M.
255. Walter Scott.
256. Byron, the poet. M.

267. Lady Sandwich.
268. Miss Lucan.
270. Pope Pius VII.
271. Cardinal Consalvi.
275-276. Prince and Princess Butera.
278 A. Marchesa Firenzi. M.
280. Heider-eddin-Gazi, rajah of Oude.
283. 303. 304 (M.). Unknown portraits.

Reliefs.

361. 363. Victory.
420. Venus, Mars, and Amor in the workshop of Vulcanus. (From the 45th song of Anacreon.)
423. Leda and the Swan.
487. Thetis dipping Achilles into the Styx.
491. Briseis led away from Achilles by the heralds of Agamemnon.
500. Hector, in the chamber of Helena, upbraiding Paris with cowardice.
504. Alexander, in triumphal car, received by the Goddess of Peace. (Variation of the centre piece of the frieze representing Alexander's triumphal procession.)
505. *Frieze.* Triumphal procession of Alexander the Great into Babylon. (Variation of the frieze in the Vestibule; in marble in villa Sommariva by the lake of Como.)
506-507. Parts of the frieze representing Alexander's triumphal procession. (For the copy in marble which was in the palace of Christiansburg.)
516. Alexander prompted by Thais to set on fire the palace at Persepolis.
526. Genius of Poetry.
529. Genius of Peace and Liberty.
551. Adam and Eve.
567. Christ at the age of twelve years teaching in the Temple.
568. Christ speaking with the woman of Samaria.

575-578. The four Evangelists, borne by the winged figures which serve as their attributes. M.
583. Luke, with his attribute, the Ox.
584. Luke as the first Christian painter.
589. Christmas-joy in Heaven.
603. The pastor Hans Madsen before the general Johan Rantzau. (Model for a bronze monument in Svanninge church, in the island of Funen.)

Sepulchral Reliefs.

593-595. Angels of the last judgement.
611. Raphael. He is crowned by the Goddess of Victory, while the Genius of Art spreads light before him.
612. Cardinal Consalvi bringing back to pope Pius VII the papal provinces. (In the Pantheon on the sarcophagus of Consalvi, together with his bust No. 271.)
613. Tobias healing his blind father. (On the tomb of the oculist Vacca Berlinghieri in the Campo Santo at Pisa.)
616. Brother and sister leaving their mother for a better world. (On the tomb of the children of Princess Poninska.)
618. Husband taking leave of his dying wife. (Over Baroness Schubart.)
620. Husband parting from his wife, who is standing before him veiled.
621. Mother leaving her son and led to the goal by the Genius of Death. (On the tomb of Countess Borchowska.)
622. The Genius of Death, standing at a funeral monument at which is kneeling an elderly woman. (Tomb of Lady Newboock.)
623. Elderly woman kneeling between two angels, one of whom is showing that life has run out, while the other is noting down its deeds. (Tomb of Lady Lawley.)

624. Woman with a cross in her hand, mounting to Heaven above the Genius of Death. (Tomb of Baroness Chandry.)
625. Similar representation.
627. Genius of Death.

CHRISTUS-HALL.

Statues.

82. Christ.
86-103. The Apostles. 86. Peter. 87. Matthew. 89. John. 91. James the less. 93. Philip. 94. Jude Thaddeus. 95. Andrew. 96. Thomas. 98. James the great. 99. Bartholomew. 101. Simon Zelotes. 103. Paul.
112. Angel of Baptism.
(These figures, except 94 and 95. are the models for the marble statues in Our Lady's Church.)

Reliefs.

559. *Frieze.* Entry of Christ into Jerusalem.
560. *Frieze.* Christ on his way to Golgotha.
(These are sketches for the friezes decorating Our Lady's Church.)
564. Christ entrusting the apostle Peter with the administration of the Church. (In marble in the chapel of the Pitti-Palace, Florence.)
569. Annunciation of the Virgin.
570. Christ, new-born, adored by the shepherds.
572. Christ, twelve years old, teaching in the Temple.
573. Christ baptized by St. John.
596. Child's Guardian Angel.
597. Christian Charity. M.
(These two reliefs are found in marble in Our Lady's Church above the school-box and the poor-box.)

ROOM I.

40. *Statue.* Ganymedes, presenting the filled cup. M.
42. — Ganymedes, filling the cup. M.
224. *Bust.* Eckersberg, Danish painter. M.
254. — Horace Vernet, the painter.
284-285. — Unknown portraits.
327. *Relief.* Genius of Light with Pegasus.
517. — Art receiving her light from the celestial Genius.
548. — Genius of the New Year.

ROOM II.

27. *Group.* Amor and Psyche reunited in Heaven. M.
426. *Relief.* The ages of Love. M.
428. — Amor leaving the couch of the sleeping Psyche.
429. — Psyche approaching the sleeping Amor with her lamp.
430. — Amor awaking the fainted Psyche. M.
585. — Singing Genii. M.
587. — Playing Genii. M.

ROOM III.

29. *Group.* The Graces and Amor.
245. *Bust.* Mrs. Rehfuss.
305. — Unknown portrait.
340. *Relief.* Apollo, the Muses and the Graces. M.
371. — Amor feeding the serpent of Hygeia. M.
375. — Amor in fetters, with the Graces. M.
393. — Amor begging Jupiter to make the Rose Queen of flowers. . M.
396. — Amor knitting a net for catching souls. M.
397. — Amor caressing the faithful dog. M.

ROOM IV.

11. *Statue.* Venus with the apple, the prize of beauty awarded to her by Paris. M.
348. *Relief.* Venus Anadyomene.
388. — Amor taming the lion.
409. — Amor drinking with Bacchus.
410. — Amor with a swan, and boys gathering fruit. (Summer.) M.
412. — Amor and the young Bacchus treading grapes. From the 17th song of Anacreon. (Autumn.) M.
414. — Amor's reception by Anacreon. From the 3d song of Anacreon. (Winter.) M.

ROOM V.

51. *Statue.* Jason with the Golden Fleece. M.
249. *Bust.* Prince Joseph Poniatowski.
286. — Unknown portrait.
489. *Relief.* Briseis led away from Achilles by the heralds of Agamemnon. M.
492 A. — Priamus supplicating Achilles for the body of Hector. M.
493. — Achilles dressing the wounds of Patroclus. M.
495. — Achilles with the killed amazon Penthesilea. M.

ROOM VI.

38. *Statue.* Hebe. M.
321. *Relief.* Hercules and Hebe. M.
322. — Æsculapius and Hygeia. M.
323. — Minerva and Prometheus. M.
324. — Nemesis and Jupiter. M.
(See p. 2 Nos. 317—320.)

ROOM VII.

6. *Group.* Mars and Amor. (From the 45th song of Anacreon.) M.

273. *Bust.* Count Sommariva.
287. -- Unknown portrait.
486. *Relief.* Perseus carrying off Andromeda on Pegasus.
499 A. — Hector with Paris and Helena. M.
501 A. — Hector's farewell to Andromache. M.
502. — Homer singing to the people.

ROOM VIII.

46. *Statue.* Goddess of Hope, with a flower in her hand. (From the ancient Greek model.) M.
366. *Relief.* The Parces with the thread of life.
367. — Night with her children, Sleep and Death. M.
368. — Day: Aurora with the Genius of Light. M.
402. — Amor summoning flowers from stony ground.
403. — Amor gathering shells for an ornament.

ROOM IX.

8. *Statue.* Vulcanus. M.
237. *Bust.* Wilhelm von Humboldt, the minister.
288. — Unknown portrait.
374. *Relief.* The Graces dancing.
418. — Amor complaining before Venus of the sting of a bee. (From the 40eth song of Anacreon.)
419. — Forging of Amor's arrows in the workshop of Vulcanus. (From the 45eth song of Anacreon.)
457. — Hymen.
497. — Ulisses receiving the arms of Achilles by the sentence of Minerva, while Ajax is withdrawing in despair. In the centre, the tomb of Achilles, on which is sitting his mother, the sea-goddess Thetis. M.

ROOM X.

4. *Statue.* Mercury on the point of killing Argus. M.
325. *Relief.* Minerva.

326. *Relief.* Apollo.
352. — Pan teaching a little Satyr to play upon the pipe of reeds. M.
354. — Bacchante with grapes, which a little Satyr is trying to reach. M.
407. — Amor with Bacchus. M.
416. — Amor with Anacreon. M.

ROOM XI.

166. *Statue.* Countess Ostermann. M.
171. — Princess Bariatinska. M.
239. *Bust.* Countess Nugent.
278. — Marchesa Firenzi.
306. — Unknown portrait.
451. *Relief.* Amor and Hymen. M.
553. — Rebecca and Eliezer at the well.
618 a. — Baroness Schubart on her death-bed. (For her tomb.) M.

ROOM XII.

124. *Statue.* Prince Joseph Poniatowski. (First model for the colossal statue in the Vestibule.)
207. *Bust.* A. P. Bernstorff, Danish minister. M.
221. — Mr. Fr. S. Vogt. M.
229. — J. C. Dahl, Norwegian landscape-painter.
234. — Prince Clemens Metternich. M.
236. — General Prince Schwarzenberg.
241. — H. Fr. Brandt, Prussian medal-engraver.
242. — C. H. Donner, merchant.
246. — The emperor Alexander I.
257. — Byron, the poet.
263. — Mr. Diwett.
272. — Count Sommariva. M.
289-290. — Unknown portraits.
316. *Relief.* Jupiter on his throne between Minerva and Nemesis. Right and left: the Goddess of the Earth and the God of the Sea.

422. *Relief.* Amor on a swan.
614. — For a sepulchral monument over Augusta Böhmer. The deceased is handing a cup of medicine to her mother. At the sides: Nemesis and the Genius of Death.
615. — For the sepulchre of Ph. Bethmann Hollweg. His brother is receiving the civic wreath of the dying youth. To the left: mother and sisters mourning. To the right: Nemesis, behind whom is seen the river-god Arno and a lion, to indicate Florence as the place of his death.
619. — For the sepulchre of Countess Pore. Husband and children of the deceased mourning.

ROOM XIII.

121. *Statue.* Lion couching. M.
130. — Byron, the poet. (In marble at Cambridge.)
210. *Bust.* H. Hielmstierne, Danish statesman.
225. — Tyge Rothe, Danish philosopher. M.
260. — Admiral Lord Exmouth.
131. *Relief.* Genius of Poetry. (Belonging to the monument of Byron.) M.
343. — Amor listening to the song of Erato. M.
357-358. — A Satyr and a Bacchante dancing.
365. — The Parces with the thread of life. M.

ROOM XIV.

44. *Statue.* Ganymedes with the eagle of Jupiter. M.
347. *Relief.* Mercury bringing the infant Bacchus to Ino.
351. — Hebe delivering the jar and the cup to Ganymedes.
389. — Amor riding on the back of the tamed lion. M.
391. — Amor writing down the laws of Jupiter. M.

417. *Relief.* Amor complaining before Venus of the sting of a bee. M.
424. — A shepherdess with a nest of Amorines. M.
484. — Hylas drawn into the river by theNymphs. M.

ROOM XV.

155. *Statue.* Prince Wladimir Potocki. (In marble over his tomb at Cracow.)
248. *Bust.* Princess Narischkin.
291. — Unknown portrait.
359. *Relief.* Victory recording heroical deeds on a shield. M.
362. — Victory with a shield and a palm-branch.
364. — Nemesis on a chariot, reining two horses, and followed by the Genii of Punishment and Reward as her train.
514. — Alexander prompted by Thais to set on fire the palace at Persepolis. M.

ROOM XVI.

22. *Statue.* Amor triumphantly examining the point of his arrow.
377-380. *Reliefs.* Amor's dominion over the world. 377. Amor in Heaven, on Jupiter's eagle, with the thunderbolt. 378. Amor on Earth, as the liontamer, with the club of Hercules. 379. Amor on the Sea, borne by a dolphin, with the trident of Neptune 380. Amor in Hades, as the tamer of Cerberus, with a fire-fork. (Also called: the four elements.) M.
395. *Relief.* Amor and Ganymedes playing at dice. (From a poem by Simonides.) M.
454. — Amor and Hymen spinning the thread of life. M.

ROOM XVII.

53 A. *Statue.* Adonis. M.
235. *Bust.* Prince Clemens Metternich.
259. — Lord Gower, duke of Sutherland.
480. *Relief.* The centaur Nessus embracing the reluctant Dejanira. M.
488.. — The centaur Chiron teaching Achilles to throw the javelin.
646. — A hunter on horseback.
647. — A huntress on horseback.

ROOM XVIII.

31. *Group.* The Graces with Amor's arrow. Behind: Cupid playing on the lyre. (The group of Room III remodelled.) M.
279. *Bust.* Vittoria from Albano.
307. — Unknown portrait.
328-336. *Reliefs.* The Muses. 328. Clio. 329. Euterpe. 330. Thalia. 331. Melpomene. 332. Terpsichore. 333. Erato. 334. Polyhymnia. 335. Urania. 336. Calliope.
337. *Relief.* The mother of the Muses, Mnemosyne, with Harpocrates.
525. — The Genii of Sculpture, Architecture, and Painting.

ROOM XIX.

176. *Statue.* Shepherd-boy. M.
406. *Relief.* Amor presenting a rose, while he is hiding thistles.
421. — Amor on a swan.
482. — Hylas drawn into the river by the Nymphs. M.
638-641. *Reliefs.* The four ages and seasons. 638. Childhood, Spring. 639. Youth, Summer. 640. Manhood, Autumn. 641. Old-age, Winter. M.

ROOM XX.

162 A. *Statue.* Thorvaldsen, leaning on the statue of Hope (see Room VII). M.
197. *Bust.* King Christian VIII, as hereditary prince.
198. — Queen Caroline Amalie, as princess.
199. — King Frederik VII, as young prince.
200. — The same, older. M.
232. — Louis I, king of Bavaria. M.
281. — Unknown portrait. M.
342. *Relief.* The Muses of Tragedy and Comedy.
518. — Art and Genius of Light.
528. — Genii of Poetry and Harmony.
601. — The Graces listening to the song of Amor. (Placed together with the medallion-portrait No. 629 on the monument of Appiani, called the painter of the Graces, in the academy at Milan.) M.

ROOM XXI.

150. *Statue.* Conradin, the last Hohenstaufe. (In marble on his tomb at Naples.)
152. — King Christian IV. (In bronze before the palace of Rosenburg, Copenhagen.)
164. — Queen Caroline Amalie, as princess.
191. *Bust.* King Frederik VI.
192. — Queen Marie Sophie Frederike.
193. — Princess Caroline, daughter of the preceding.
196. — Princess Vilhelmine Marie, likewise.
201. — Prince Fr. Wilhelm of Hesse-Philipsthal.
202. — Princess Juliane, his wife.
557. *Relief.* Baptism of Christ.
558. — Institution of the Lord's Supper.
563. — Christ and his two disciples at Emmaus.
599. — Christian Charity united with Faith and Hope.

UPPER FLOOR.

Thorvaldsen's works, Pictures, Drawings, Antiquities, Casts of antiques, Books, &c.*)

STAIRCASE.

14. *Statue.* Hercules. (Model for one of the four bronze statues before the palace of Christiansburg.)
308. *Bust.* Unknown portrait.
398. *Relief.* Amor knitting a net for catching souls.
399. — Amor caressing the faithful dog.
450. — Amor and Psyche.
452. — Amor and Hymen.
456. — Amor flying away.
520. — Genius of Painting.
521. — Genius of Architecture.
522-523. — Genius of Sculpture.
527. — Genius of Poetry.

CORRIDOR.

Statues.

2. Bacchus.
3. Apollo.
5. Mercury on the point of killing Argus.

---

*) Sculptures, not cited as the works of others or as casts of antiques, are by Thorvaldsen.

12. Venus with the apple.
24. Amor triumphant.
26. Psyche with the urn.
28. Reunion of Amor and Psyche.
32. The Graces and Amor.
34. Amor, sitting, with the lyre.
36. Amor, standing, with the bow.
37. 39. Hebe. (No. 39 is a remodelling of No. 37.)
41. Ganymedes presenting the filled cup.
43. Ganymedes filling the cup.
45. Ganymedes with the eagle of Jupiter.
47. Goddess of Hope.
53. Adonis.
132. Byron, the poet.
167. Countess Ostermann.
172. Princess Bariatinska.
173. Georgiana Russel.
174. A little girl, represented as Psyche.
177. A shepherd-boy.
178. 179. Female dancers.
181. A dancing girl.

Busts.

190. Ludvig Holberg, the Danish author.
213. Admiral H. Holsten.
215. Countess H. Danneskiold.
217. Baroness Chr. Stampe.
218. Miss Ida Brun.
222. Mr. Fr. S. Vogt.
226. Adam Öhlenschläger, the Danish poet.
227. Mr. Bartholin Eichel.
238. Countess Dietrichstein.
243. Baron Eichthal.
250. Princess Bariatinska.
251. Countess Potocka.
262. Mr. Alex. Baillie.
264. Mrs. Hope.

269. Miss Lucan.
274. Count Sommariva.
277. Giov. Torlonia, duke of Bracciano.
294. Sir Henry Labouchère.
292, 293, 295-300, 309-313. Unknown portraits.

Reliefs.

134. Genius of Poetry.
339. Procession to Parnassus. Apollo with Pegasus and the Genius of Light; the Graces and the Muses with Amorines; Homer led by the Genius of Poetry.
341. Apollo, the Muses, and the Graces on Parnassus.
347. Mercury bringing the infant Bacchus to Ino.
353. Pan and a little Satyr.
355. A Bacchante and a little Satyr.
356, 356 A. A lascivious Pan and a Nymph of the chase. (No. 356 A: M.)
360. Victory.
369, 370. Night. Day.
372. Hygeia and Amor.
376. Amor fettered by the Graces.
381-84. Amor's dominion over the world.
385-86. Amor on Jupiter's eagle
387, 387 A. Amor with the tamed lion. (Nr. 387 A: M.)
390. Amor on the back of the lion.
392. Amor writing down the laws of Jupiter.
394. Amor begging Jupiter to make the Rose Queen of flowers.
400. Amor sailing.
404. Amor setting the stone on fire.
408. Amor with Bacchus.
411. Summer.
413. Autumn. (Amor and the infant Bacchus.)
415. Winter. (Amor with Anacreon.)
417 a. Amor complaining to Venus of the sting of a bee.
431. Amor awakening the fainted Psyche.
433-48. Representations from the myth of Amor and Psyche.

455. Amor and Hymen spinning the thread of life.
458-79. Various mythological representations. 458. Latona fleeing. 459. Diana with her hind. 460-61. Diana and Actæon. 462-63. Diana and Orion. 464. Chione and Dædalion. 465-66. Diana and Endymion. 467-71. Diana's Nymphs. 472. Callisto. 473. Atalanta. 474. Meleager. 475. A hero with a slain lion. 476. Adonis. 477. Narcissus. 478. Apollo and Daphne. 479. Pan with his flute Syrinx.
481. Nessus and Dejanira.
483. 485. Hylas caught by the River-Nymphs.
490. Briseis carried away from Achilles.
492. Priamus and Achilles.
494. Achilles and Patroclus.
496. Achilles and Penthesilea.
498. Minerva awarding the arms of Achilles to Ulisses.
499. Hector with Paris and Helena.
501. Hector taking leave from Andromache.
508. *Frieze.* Alexander's triumphal procession, on a reduced scale and with variations. (See Vestibule.) M.
509. Variation of the middle part of the preceding frieze. M.
510-11. Parts of the model for the same frieze.
512-13. Additions to the same.
515. Alexander prompted to set Persepolis on fire.
532-45. Genii of: Poetry 532, Tragedy 533, Comedy 534, Music 535, Dancing 536, State-Government 537, War 538, Navigation 539, Trade 540, Medicine 541, Gardening 542, Agriculture 543, Astronomy 544, Religion 545.
549. Justice.
556. Mary with the infant Christ and St. John.
562. Christ and the two disciples at Emmaus.
565. Christ entrusting St. Peter with the government of the Church.
571. Mary's flight from the murder of the innocents at Bethlehem.
579-82. The four Evangelists.

586. Angels singing.
588. Angels playing.
590-92. Angels with flowers and garlands.
602. The Graces and Amor.
626. Genius of Death. M.
628. Praying children.
629. The painter Appiani.
631. The painter G. B. Bassi.
632. Göthe (son af the poet).
633. The philosopher Henrik Stephens.
635. Unknown portrait.
636, 637. Family scenes. Thorvaldsen with the family of Stampe at Nysö. Baron Stampe and his sons on the beach.
642-45. The ages of life and the seasons of the year.

ROOM XXII.

194. *Bust.* Vilhelmine Marie, Danish princess.
261. — Lord W. Bentinck.
265-66. — Sons af Sir Thomas Hope.
405. *Relief.* Amor with roses and thistles.

Paintings.

68. *Castelli.* Landscape with a castle on a rock. (Sketch.)
100. *Severn.* Vintage-jollity.
101. *Williams.* Children in the Roman Campagna.
120. *Hering.* Street in Smyrna.
134. *Öhme.* Part of the exterior of a Gothic church.
155. *J. Riepenhausen.* A second-hand bookseller in a street at Rome.
184-85. *J. C. Dahl.* Norwegian landscapes.
190. *Fearnley.* Norwegian waterfall.
243. *A. Küchler.* Correggio's death. (From the tragedy of Öhlenschläger.)
269. *E. Meyer.* A Neapolitan fisherman in his doorway.
273. — A young Franciscan friar.

ROOM XXIII.

1. *Group.* Bacchus and Ariadne.
373. *Relief.* Hygeia crowned by Amor.

Paintings.

62. *Bassi.* A path in a wood.
79. *Fioroni.* Pope Pius VIII carried in procession through the colonnade of St. Peter's church.
99. *Severn.* An Italian peasant-woman with her sleeping daughter.
116. *Foltz.* Blind beggar girl sleeping at the entrance of a Roman church.
129. *Koch.* Noah's offering after the Flood.
136. *Overbeck.* Mary with the infant Christ.
138. *Rebell.* Coast-view from the island of Capri.
142. *Reinhart.* Roman landscape. (The motive taken from Torre del Quinto.)
143. — Landscape; in the foreground, a hunter reposing.
154. *J. Riepenhausen.* Raphael introduced by Bramante to pope Julius II.
177, 179. *J. C. Dahl.* The bay of Naples by moonlight.
246. *A. Küchler.* Roman citizen-folks buying an abbate-hat for their little son.
265. *Anton Melbye.* Fishing boats in the Channel.
266. *E. Meyer.* A public writer in a street at Rome reading a letter to a peasant-girl.
267. — The same writing a letter for her.
270. — A fisherman in the island of Capri.
296. *Thöming.* Coast-view in Capri.

ROOM XXIV.

23. *Statue.* Amor triumphant, regarding his arrow. M.
214. *Bust.* Count Chr. Danneskiold.
216. — Countess L. Danneskiold.
346. *Relief.* Mercury bringing the infant Bacchus to Ino.

Paintings.

56. *Voogd.* Italian landscape.
91. *Labouère.* The coast of the Pontine marshes.
93. *Leopold Robert.* A young Greek whetting his poniard.
122. *Hopfgarten.* Transformation of the bread of St. Elisabeth of Thuringia into roses.
139-40. *Reinhardt.* Groups of trees.
156. *W. Schadow.* Christ on his way to Golgotha:
183. *J. C. Dahl.* A waterfall. (Sketch.)
201. *Buntzen.* Danish landscape.
202. — Part of the garden of Villa Borghese near Rome.
220. *Constantin Hansen.* Part of the temple of Neptune by Pæstum.
247. *A. Küchler.* A little abbate, being heard his lesson by his sister.
251. *J. L. Lund.* St. Anna teaching St. Mary to read.
291. *J. V. Sonne.* Battle-field, the morning after the battle.
293. *Thöming.* Danish corvette in the Sound.
299. *Catel* and *Rubbi*, after *Carstens.* The Golden Age.

ROOM XXV.

173 A. *Statue.* Georgiana Russel. M.
401. *Relief.* Amor sailing.

Paintings.

102. *Teerlink.* Landscape with cattle.
103. — Italian landscape.
124. *Klenze.* The town of Pirano in Istria.
126. *Koch.* Italian landscape. (Free composition.)
127. — Olevano in the Sabine mountains.
141. *Reinhardt.* Ponte Lupo by Tivoli.
148. *Richter.* A Roman woman. (Fortunata.)
149. — Roman woman with a tambourine.
159. *Schilbach.* View over the Forum of Rome up to the Capitol.

160. *Schilbach.* View from the Capitol over the Forum.
172-73. *Marko.* Italian mountain-landscapes.
187. *J. C. Dahl.* Entrance to the harbour of Copenhagen.
197. *Bendz.* Evening-assembly of artists at a coffee-house in Munich.
199. *Blunck.* Thorvaldsen among Danish artists in a Roman osteria.
240. *Kierschou.* Part of the road between Rammsau and Reichenhall in Bavarian Tyrol.
263. *Ant. Melbye.* Ships off the coast on a calm morning.
282. *Petzholdt.* Site of the ancient Veii.

ROOM XXVI.

180. *Statue.* Young girl dancing. M.
208. *Bust.* A. P. Bernstorff.
228. — Mother of the painter Chr. F. Höyer.
345. *Relief.* Diana entreating Jupiter that she may remain a virgin.

Paintings.

67. *Camuccini.* Christ blessing the children.
82. *Gazzarini.* Christ new-born.
86. *Pacetti.* Copy after *Bassi.* The grotto of Posilippo in the neigbourhood of Naples.
95. *Horace Vernet.* Thorvaldsen working at Vernet's bust.
118. *C. v. Heideck.* Scene from the defence of a beseiged Spanish town.
133. *Nerly.* Buffaloes drawing a block of marble to Rome for the atelier of Thorvaldsen.
151. *Riedel.* Girl bathing.
166. *Weller.* Jugglers before the Marcellus-Theatre atRome.
204. *Buntzen.* Danish landscape.
214. *Eckersberg.* St. Peter's place in Rome.
215. — Mary with the infant Christ in the clouds.
231. *J. L. Jensen.* Fruits.
232. — Flowers in a vase.

252. *J. L. Lund.* Italian landscape.
255. *Lundbye.* Tomb from the »Stone-Age« on Refsnæs in Sealand.
264. *Ant. Melbye.* Ships in a fresh gale.
272. *E. Meyer.* A friar with a money-box.
275. *Mohr.* View from the neighbourhood of Isseldorf in Bavaria.

ROOM XXVII.

33. *Statue.* Amor playing on a lyre. M.
338. *Relief.* The Graces.

Paintings.

60. *Bassi.* Groups of trees by some water.
125. *Koch.* A landscape. Inserted figures: Apollo among the shepherds.
145. *Reinhold.* Mountainous landscape. Inserted figures: the good Samaritan.
147. — Prospect of St. Peter's church.
153. *J. Riepenhausen.* Amor and two young girls.
164. *Tischbein.* Neapolitan fisher-girl.
178. 180. *J. C. Dahl.* Bay of Naples by moonlight.
181. — Place of St. Peter by moonlight.
230. *J. L. Jensen.* Flowers.
233. — A kitchen-dresser.
234. — A vase with flowers.
242. *Krafft.* Carnival-scene in a Roman street.
280. *Ottesen.* Fruits.
281. — A breakfast-table.

ROOM XXVIII.

301. *Bust.* Count Coronini-Cronberg.
302. — Unknown portrait.
555. *Reliefs* for a Christening Font: Baptism of Christ; Mary with the infant Saviour and St. John; Christ blessing the children; three hovering angels.

Paintings.

61. *Bassi.* A road between Italian villas. (Terni.)
63. — A view of the ruins of the palaces of the Emperors in Rome.
70. *Diofebi.* Entrance of the church of Sta. Maria in ara celi, Rome.
85. *Storelli.* Italian town in the mountains.
110. *Catel.* A grotto in the villa of Mæcenas at Tivoli.
111. — Night-piece. From the closing scene in Chateaubriand's tale of René.
135. *Oppenheim.* Return of Tobias.
157. *Schick.* Landscape with antique buildings.
158. *Schick* and *Koch.* Landscape; in the fore-ground. Boaz and Ruth in the field.

163a. *Rudolf Suhrlandt.* Thorvaldsen (in his 40eth year).

163b. — Canova (in his 54th year).

198. *Blunck.* Noah in the Ark.
256. *Lunde.* View of the Palace of Frederiksberg.
259. *Martens.* The hall of antiques in Charlottenburg at Copenhagen.
268. *E. Meyer.* Fisher-man in Capri.
276. *Adam Müller.* Christ and the Evangelists.
289. *Schleisner.* Shoemaker's apprentices playing tricks upon their master during his sleep.
292. *J. V. Sonne.* Roman country-folk before the osteria of Ponte Mammolo.
294. *Thöming.* The bay of Naples.

ROOM XXIX.

35. Amor with his bow, standing. M.

Paintings.

84. *Lazzarini.* Part of the aqueduct Aqua Virgo in Rome.
87. *Chauvin.* View in the garden of Villa Falconieri near Frascati.
88. — View in the garden of Villa d'Este at Tivoli.
89. — Grotta Ferrata in the Albano-hills.

92. *Leopold Robert.* Church of St. Paolo outside Rome, the day after the fire in 1823.
104. *Verstappen.* A chapel on the road to Ariccia.
130. *Lindau.* Country-people on their way to Rome.
131. — Saltarello at a Roman osteria.
150. *Riedel.* Neapolitan fisherman's family.
161. *Senf.* Flowers in an antique vase.
209. *Eckersberg.* A sleeping woman.
211. — A Roman beggar.
250. *Libert.* Heath-country in Jutland.
275a. *Monies.* Scene in a kitchen.
277. *J. P. Möller.* The sound by the town of Svendborg.
278. — The town of Svendborg.
279. Miss *Neergaard.* Flowers in a glass.
295. *Thöming.* Bay of Naples.

ROOM XXX.

244. *Bust.* Mrs. Krause.
282. 314. 315. *Busts.* Unknown portraits.

Paintings.

80. *De Francesco.* Italian landscape.
97. *Lazzarini.* Copy after *Granet.* The choir of the Capuchin-convent at the Piazza Barberina at Rome.
106. *Bürkel.* Country-people before a Roman osteria.
107. — A bear-leader in a Roman village.
113. *Cornelius.* Interment of Christ.
117. *Foltz.* Composition after the poem of Uhland: The Minstrel's Curse.
119. *Henning.* Head of an Italian woman. (Fortunata.)
123. *Kaufmann.* Country-people outside a Tyrolese inn.
152. *J. Riepenhausen.* Adonis leaving Venus to go a-hunting.
175. *Kiprenski.* Armenian priest. (Study.)
186. *J. C. Dahl.* Norwegian mountain landscape.
241. *Kloss.* Approach from the sea-side to Copenhagen.

258. *Marstrand.* Amusements outside the walls of Rome on an October-evening.
298. *Thöming.* Surf on the coast of Capri. (Study.)

ROOM XXXI.

25. *Statue.* Psyche with the urn. M.
432. *Relief.* Psyche carried to Heaven by Mercury. (Sketch.)

Paintings.

78. *Fioroni.* The host of the osteria in the place Della trinità de' monti at Rome, acting as improvisatore.
81. *De Francesco.* Italian landscape. Inserted figures: Æneas meeting the Sibyl.
83. *Landesio.* Italian landscape.
90. *Gudin.* Neapolitan coast.
94. *Horace Vernet.* Armenian priest. (Study.)
109. *Catel.* Neapolitan fisher-family.
146. *Reinhold.* Mountain-landscape. Inserted figures: Hagar and Ishmael.
162. *Steingrübel.* View of Florence.
169. *Marko.* View from a grotto to the Monte Cavo in the Albano-hills.
170. 171. — Landscapes with Nymphs of the chase.
200. *Boesen.* Danish woody landscape.
210. *Eckersberg.* A reaping woman in antique dress.
212. — Socrates and Alcibiades.
218. *Friedländer.* Fishermen in a Danish fisher-village assembled round a draught of herrings.
244. *A. Küchler.* Family-scene at Albano.
258a. *Marstrand.* A Roman abbate jesting with young girls.
271. *E. Meyer.* The Franciscan convent near Amalfi.
285a. *Roed.* Portrait of the painter A. Küchler when a monk.
286. *Rörbye.* View of Athens; in the fore-ground, Greeks in conversation.

ROOM XXXII.

230. *Bust.* Mr. J. Knudtzon.
231. -- Mr. H C. Knudtzon.
425. *Relief.* A shepherdess with a nest full of Amorines.
598. — Christian Charity.
630. — The physician Vacca Berlinghieri (?).
634. — Mr. E. H. Löffler.

Paintings.

96. *Giovannini.* A chemist in his laboratory.
114. *Elsasser.* View from the ruins of the theatre at Taormina.
128. *Koch* and *Dahl.* View of the Jungfrau in Switzerland.
167. *Wittmer.* Æsop telling his fables.
253. *Lundbye.* Tract by the lake of Arresö in Sealand.
254. — Neigbourhood of Frederiksværk in Sealand.
287. *Rörbye.* View of Piazza marina at Palermo.

*Drawings.**)

ROOM XXXIII.

Sketches for Statues and Monuments.

10. Vulcanus.
13. Venus and Amor.
15-16. Hercules.
17-18. Minerva.
19-19 a. Nemesis.
20-21. Æsculapius.
30. The Graces.
48. Victory.
49-50. Triumphant Muse.
57-58. Sibyls.
73-81. Figures for the representation of the preaching of John the Baptist.

*) Various drawings are from time to time exposed in the frames i this and in the next room.

83-85. Christ.
88-109. Apostles.
111-112 a. Angels of Baptism.
117. Gutenberg.
120. For a monument over general Schwarzenberg.
126. Poniatowski.
127. Maximilian I of Bavaria.
133. Byron.
138. Schiller.
139-40. Göthe.
141. Frederik VI.
148-49. For the monument over pope Pius VII.
151. Conradin of Naples.
157. Genii of life and death.
158. The same at a Meta.
159. Kneeling angel.
160. Luther.
161. Melanchton.
163. Thorvaldsen.
168-70. Ladies, sitting.
175. A young hunter.
177 a. A shepherd boy.
178 a. Female dancer,
182. A young girl dancing.
184. A flower girl.
185. A youth with a dog.

Reliefs, mostly sketches.

118. Inventing of the printing press. (For the pedestal of Gutenberg's statue.)
153. Three Genii representing the motto of Christian IV: Regna firmat pietas. (For the pedestal of the statue of this king.)
344. Apollo among the shepherds.
427. The various ages of Love.
546-47. Genii of Arts and Trades.
552. Adam and Eve.

554. Solomon's judgement.
561. Resurrection of Christ.
566. Christ blessing the Children.
604-7. The abolition of villanage; the institution of provincial assemblies; the exercise of justice; the protection of arts and sciences. (For the monument of Frederik VI.)
609. Justice and Strength. (For the same monument.)
617. For the sepulchral monument of the two Poninsky, brother and sister.

Collection of Drawings and Engravings. Library.

ROOM XXXIV.

649. Marble chimney-piece with two Caryatides and a frieze of Amorines, after Thorvaldsen.

Relief Sketches.

349-50. Rape of Ganymedes.
449. Amor and Psyche.
453. Amor tying together the torches of Hymen.
550. Denmark praying for the king.
574. Entry of Christ into Jerusalem.
608. The abolition of villanage. (For the monument of Frederik VI.)
610. Symbols of Arts and Sciences, crowned by Genii. (For the same monument.)
648. A young girl with a bird.

Casts of Antique Statues.

30. Apollo of Belvedere.
31. Apollo (Apollino), in Florence.
32. The Medicean Venus.
33. The Capitolian Venus.
36. Amor and Psyche, at the Capitol.
38. Mercury, in the Vatican.

40. Silenus with Bacchus, in the Louvre.
47. A victorious athlete (hoplitodrome), in the Louvre.
48. The discus-thrower, in the Vatican.

ROOM XXXV.

Egyptian Antiquities.

Case 1 and Montres 2-3. Images of deities and holy animals, religious symbols, amulets, and signets.

Case 4. Vases, jars, and various other vessels for domestic use.

Montres 5-6. Finger-rings, pearls, fragments of glass work, sistrum-handles, a doll, a mirror, a rouge-box, &c.

Case 7. Sepulchral stones, tablets, and figures.

Montres 8-9. Mummy-ornaments. Breast-plates and scarabees from mummies.

Below: Grave-urns.

Plaster casts of two statues of kings and of the lid of a sarcophagus.

Books.

ROOM XXXVI.

Greek, Etruscan, and Roman Antiquities.

Case 1. Small bronze figures, some of them representing gods, others men.

Montres 2-3. Bronze ornaments exhibiting figures and heads of gods, men, animals &c.

Case 4. Etruscan bronze mirrors, with engraved figures on the reverse.

Montres 5-6. Finger-rings, amulet-capsules, buckles, head-, neck-, and arm-rings, hair-pins, weights, keys, spoons, surgical instruments &c., of bronze.

Case 7. Vessels, lamps, a candelabrum, bells, strigils, weapons, utensils &c., of bronze.

Case 8. Kitchen-utensils, salve-vases, handles and feet of vessels, of bronze.

Montre **9.** Ivory and bone work: dice, a theatre-ticket, a gladiator-tessera, needles, a doll, &c.

Montre **10.** Amulets, ornaments and small fragments of vases, made of hard or precious stones. Amulets and ornaments of silver. Tickets and other objects of lead.

Case **11.** A bowl, a jug, oil-flasks &c., of glass. A Jupiter's-head in ivory. A Roman portrait-head in silver.

Montre **12.** Glass ornaments. Fragments of glass-tablets with figures in relief, used as ornaments of walls and ceilings.

Montre **13.** Gold ornaments: finger-rings, ear-rings, buckles, amulets, a bracelet, a necklace &c.

Books.

ROOM XXXVII.

Antique Gems and Pastes.

Hard and precious stones with engraved figures (*gems, intaglios*) and antique glass casts (*pastes*) of such, Etruscan, Greek, and Roman. I. Scarabees, mostly Etruscan, Nos. 1—59. Among these are to be noted Nos. 1, 2, 16, 17, 19, 20, 26, 53, and 54, on account of the well cut figures. II. Older style of art, Nos. 60—81. Among these Nos. 60—62, 70—72, 76, and 77 are remarkable for careful workmanship. III. Productions of the developed Greek and Roman art, Nos. 82—1583. Deities, Nos. 82—786. Heroes, Nos. 787—965. Representations from history, Nos. 966—1084. Human occupations, Nos. 1085—1300. Animals, Nos. 1301—1496. Symbolical and phantastical representations, Nos. 1497—1583 Stones of this class more particularly worthy of notice on account of artistical value are the following. Of those set in gold: Nos. 89, 104, 188, 295, 296. 323, 360, 388, 408, 411, 495, 643, 851, 980, 990, 992, 993, 995, 1003, 1042, 1169, 1203—5, 1224, 1248,, 1263, 1265, 1274, 1359, 1362, 1364, 1377, 1383, 1504. Of those not set: Nos. 133, 461, 530, 583, 641, 760, 796, 819, 949, 999, 1007, 1194, 1245, IV. Works of declining art, Nos. 1584—1693. — The gold rings of Nos. 2, 40, 44, 56, 388, 661, and 1053 are antique, the rest modern.

Cut stones with relief-work (*cameos*) and antique glass imitations of such, Nos. 1—133. Through their artistical execution are distinguished: Nos. 16, 32, 42, 53, 58, 59, 72, 81 ,89, 97, 103, 128.

ROOM XXXVIII.

Antique Coins.

I. Greek Coins from Europe, Asia, and Africa. A. Before the middle of the 5th century b. C. B. From the middle of the 5th century until the Roman empire. C. From the times of the Roman Empire. II. Coins of the Persians, Phenicians, Carthagenians, Celtiberians, and Barbarians of Gaul and Germany. III. Coins of Roman colonies. A. During the Republic, B. During the Empire. IV. Coins of the Roman state. A. During the Republic. B. During the Empire. V. Byzantine coins.

Modern Medals.

Montre at the window. Nos. 1—14. Medals stamped in honour of Thorvaldsen. Nos. 15—25. Medals with representations borrowed from his works or for which he has executed the models. Nos. 32—35. The four prize medals of the Danish Academy of Arts gained by Thorvaldsen. Nos. 26—31 and 36—134. Other medals from different countries.

Paintings.

Nos. 1—4. Florentine paintings in distemper from the 14th and 15th centuries. No. 5. Bolognese from the 16th century. No. 8. Florentine from the 16th century. No. 16. Sassoferrato. No. 20. Guercino. No. 21. Bolognese from the 17th century. Nos. 35—38. Copies after Raphael.

On the case in the back-ground, which contains the rest of the collection of antique coins, stands Thorvaldsen's bust in marble by Tenerani.

ROOM XXXIX.

Antique Sculptures of Marble and Terra-cotta.

Right Sidewall (from the door of the corridor). Marbles. Heads of Satyrs, Pan, Vertumnus, the emperor Hadrian apotheosized, and private Romans. A male torso. Architectural fragments. A Roman sepulchral tablet and *cista.* Fragments of a Grecian tombstone, a Roman sarcophagus, and several reliefs.

Case **1.** Marbles. Statuettes, or torsos and heads of statuettes: Cybele, Minerva, the Ephesian Diana, Amor, the bearded Bacchus, Satyrs, Æsculapius, Flora &c. Fragments of various other sculptures.

Case **2.** Terra-cotta. Small figures and heads, being representations of gods and men.

Left Sidewall. Terra-cotta. On the cornice: Various ornaments of roofs. In the wall: Fragments of architectural relief-slabs. Below: 3 slabs of a frieze representing the deeds of Hercules.

Montres **3-4.** Roman lamps. **5.** Small figures and heads, fragments of Aretinian vessels &c., of terra-cotta.

ROOM XL.

Antique Vases of Terra-Cotta.

Painted Greek vases. I. From the first period (7—6th centuries b. C.) or in the oldest style of such vase-fabrication, with brown and violet figures and ornaments on a pale yellowish ground. Nos. 1—8, in case **1.** II. From the second period (6—5th centuries b. C.) or in the so-called archaic style, with black figures and ornaments on a light reddish ground: Nos. 10 - 90, in cases **1** and **2.** III. From the best period of Greek art (5—4th centuries b. C.), in beautiful style; with light reddish figures on black ground: Nos. 92—129, in the two upper compartments of cases **3** and **4.** IV. From the last period, that of the decline of this fabrication

(3d and following centuries b. C.), likewise with light reddish figures and ornaments on black ground: Nos. 130—148, in the lowest compartment of cases **3** and **4**.

Pottery without painting, Etruscan, Italian, and Greek, in the lowest compartment of cases **1—2**.

ROOM XLI.

Libray.

Plaster casts of Antique Busts.

139. Euripides. 140. Menander. 141. Posidippus. 145. Lysias. 148. Themistocles. 158. Cn. Domitius Corbulo.

Paintings.

132. *Magnus.* Portrait of Thorvaldsen.
217. *Eckersberg.* Arrival of Thorvaldsen on the road of Copenhagen, Sept. 17. 1838.

ROOM XLII.

Thorvaldsen's last unfinished works.

188. Bust of Luther.
524. Chalk-drawing for a relief. The Genius of Sculpture sitting on the shoulder of a statue of Jupiter.

Paintings.

108. *Carus.* Ancient tomb by moonlight.
144. *Reinhardt.* View of Mount Vesuvius.
163. *Stieler.* Louis I of Bavaria, as crown prince.
168. *Koop*, copy after *Begas.* Thorvaldsen.
188-189. *J. C. Dahl.* Norwegian landscapes.
203. *Buntzen.* Nysö in Sealand. (Summer-residence of Thorvaldsen.)
205. *Bærentsen.* Mrs. Heiberg, Danish actress.
216. *Eckersberg.* King Frederik VI.
216 a. *Eckersberg.* Thorvaldsen.

220 a. *C. Hansen.* Bindesböll, the architect of the museum.

220 b. — Mr. J. Collin, President of the Direction of the museum.

227. *A. Jensen.* Fritzsch, Danish flower-painter.

245. *A. Küchler.* Colonel Paulsen and his wife, a daughter of Thorvaldsen, with their childern.

258 b. *V. Marstrand.* J. M. Thiele, the biographer of Thorvaldsen.

285. *F. Richardt.* Thorvaldsen in his atelier at Copenhagen.

311. *Balsgaard*, copy after *A. Jensen.* H. Freund, Danish sculptor. (On porcelain.)

Thorvaldsen's bust by *V. Bissen.*

Chamber-clock in a case, the wooden work of which has been carved by Thorvaldsen in his youth.

Thorvaldsen's furniture (from his dwelling at Copenhagen).